BORN FIGHTING
AN UPHILL BATTLE

THE MISUNDERSTOOD BLACK MALE

BY

KEITH HORTON

USA ▪ Canada ▪ UK ▪ Ireland

Cover illustration by Karin Huggens and Type treatment by Zenon Slawinski
Editor–Melanie Rigney

Note for Librarians: A cataloguing record for this book is available from Library
and Archives Canada at www.collectionscanada.ca/amicus/index-e.html
ISBN 1-4251-0515-7

PUBLISHING™

Offices in Canada, USA, Ireland and UK

Book sales for North America and international:
Trafford Publishing, 6E–2333 Government St.,
Victoria, BC V8T 4P4 CANADA
phone 250 383 6864 (toll-free 1 888 232 4444)
fax 250 383 6804; email to orders@trafford.com
Book sales in Europe:
Trafford Publishing (UK) Limited, 9 Park End Street, 2nd Floor
Oxford, UK OX1 1HH UNITED KINGDOM
phone +44 (0)1865 722 113 (local rate 0845 230 9601)
facsimile +44 (0)1865 722 868; info.uk@trafford.com
Order online at:
trafford.com/06-2273

10 9 8 7 6 5 4 3 2

Contents

"Born Fighting an Uphill Battle"
The Misunderstood Black Male

Introduction

"In childhood, be modest; in youth, temperate; in adulthood, just; and in old age, prudent." ~Socrates~

YOU FEEL LIKE your back is against the wall and people just don't understand you. As a matter of fact, your parent or parents just don't understand why you act the way you do. People are constantly telling you horror stories about a person they know who is strung out on drugs or was shot and killed or who is serving time in jail... and you say to yourself, what the heck does that have to do with me? This book is about you, the black boy, and what you can do to prove them wrong.

In this book, I'm not going to pull any punches, I'm going to be straightforward and say everything that I tell my son and the twenty-five or so young men whom I've mentored over the past three years... I mean everythang.

~The Scenario~

YOU WERE BORN somewhere in the United States in the '90s to a proud parent or parents. Trust me on this one… you are blessed to be a citizen of this country. You already have an upper hand over the four or five billion other folks in the world. Don't get too excited, though, because from your birth you are fighting an uphill battle in life that even your future wife, girlfriend, or mother will not experience. Your struggle cannot be identified with anyone except another black male who has traveled the path that you are about to travel.

You may have grown up with two parents in the house and seen your kinfolk every now and then. You may have grown up with sisters and brothers and had to share everything you had. You may be a foster child and living with folks whom you may or may not like. If you weren't fortunate enough to know your parent or parents, it's all right because you have something in you that makes you a survivor. Whatever your situation, you are a black boy on this planet and are not the first to go through the trials that you will experience in this country.

Your mama, big mama, grandma or nana took care of you when you were young and made sure that you had the best clothes… the little Air Nikes when you couldn't even walk. They showered you with love and attention. They may have read a book or two to you during your preschool years, but I doubt it. They may have taken you to church to get you off to a good start but more than likely, you went only every now and then.

They let you play outside when your chores or homework was done because that's what boys are supposed to do. However, you lied at least once that your chores or homework was done so that you could go outside. Everyone in your family wanted to know what type of skills you had, so they enrolled you in basketball, flag football, soccer, or T-ball before you were even six. It didn't matter if you were chubby, fat, or punkish looking; they put you in there to see what you could do.

Your parents may or may not have been daycare savvy. They had to work to maintain their lifestyle and a nice environment for you. They enrolled you in a daycare center that was affordable, clean, and safe. The daycare center was supposed to complement the basics you were getting at home but more than likely, the center was the primary source of education. Education was not necessarily the primary focus at the daycare center. Maintaining a safe and clean place took priority and more than likely, the staff did a magnificent job of keeping you clean and safe.

You may have missed some of the basics that were needed to keep you up to par with the other students, so now it will be up to you and your parent or parents to catch you up. Your journey uphill has just begun.

At a very early age, your uncles bragged on you that you were going to be tall or strong or be a good football player or basketball player. They said, "Look at those hands; he is definitely going to be wide receiver" or "Look at those legs, he is going to be a track star." They may have even narrowed it down further; since you had long legs, they may have predicted that you would race in the 400-meter run. Your aunts compared you to other males in the family and said, "The girls better watch out" or "He is going to be fine just like Big Daddy."

~The Curve Ball in First Grade~

DO YOU KNOW what a curve ball is? A curve ball is when someone throws something at you that is not straight, not fair, something that you can't judge... most people miss the curve balls. Do you hear me? Your first curve ball is thrown to you the day you enter grade or elementary school. Your teacher, Mrs. Downing, a white lady about forty-five years old who doesn't live in your neighborhood and doesn't understand black folks, looks at you when you walk in the classroom. She looks at what you have on and makes up her mind about you. If you don't or didn't have a Mrs. Downing, then you may have a Mrs. Washington, a black teacher who divorced her no-good black husband. She is pissed off at all black men and you just happen to remind her of her ex-husband. She ain't going to cut you no slack and, as matter of fact, she may be harder on you than any of the other kids in your room. Believe me, you will have a Mrs. Downing or Washington during your schooling. But you will also have very good teachers who care about you.

You take your seat as directed by the teacher and immediately begin checking out your surroundings. You look at your potential competition during recess and see how you can impress the other kids in your class. You tell yourself that you have to fit in, and the only way you can do it is by being cool or good at sports. Your mama has told you to do your best during school, but that doesn't mean anything to you because all you need to do is to get a passing grade, C or better, and show the kids that you have skills and you will be like gold. You ain't trying to be no bookworm, that's for them little white boys and girls. Heck, if you try to do well, then they are going to think you are trying to act white or be some kinda geek... all you want is a passing grade or good enough so that you can play.

STOP Did you miss the curve ball? Are you still sitting on the bench? A lot of teachers have been conditioned to think that black boys cannot achieve at the same level as the white boys or especially girls. From your birth, you have been programmed to think that black boys are only good at sports and that As and Bs are for white folks and black girls. You are already a step behind your peers. It's not really your parents' fault; they were trying to get you involved and active.

Did you notice when you played soccer that they told you to do the running and kicking and not play goalie? Did you notice that when you played flag football you played running back, maybe even quarterback because they wanted somebody to run fast? Did you notice how the black and white coaches fought over the black boys who

they thought could run fast or jump high? In school, how many teachers fought over having you on the spelling team or in honors classes? Did they even consider you?

Life is a game, and you are not even stepping up to hit the curve ball. You know what? They don't give a care if you step up or not; you ain't hurting no one but yourself. Do you know that black kids make up half of the slow classes or learning disability classes in the United States? I speculate that 82 percent of the blacks in those classes are black boys? Here is a shocker… do you know that over half of the 82 percent of black boys in those classes should not be there and should be in regular classes? Let me break it down further: if you had a hundred kids in slow classes or learning disabled classes, about fifty will be black and out of that fifty, forty-one will be black boys. You think they really care? What are you going to do about it?

What do you do if you have no athletic skills? You are in a trick now, because the alternative is to do well in school and that means that people will label you as a white boy, trying to act white, nerd, geek, or punk. As a matter of fact, you really like drawing or want to be an actor, but what will people think of you if you let them know that?

STOP **Here's the truth: to heck with them. You have to live your life for you, not them. Are you trying to make them happy or fit in, or are you trying to set yourself up so that you can become successful in life? You tell yourself that you ain't going to be no crackhead, broke negro, in jail or shot and killed, but if you continue to live your life to please your friends, then you are more likely to fall into one of these categories.**

You tell yourself that you don't care about school because you will be a star basketball player or football player. You will play in the NFL or NBA or become a music producer or maybe a rapper. You say that because that's all you know. You have no clue what you have to do to become something other than a sports idol or rapper. If you have a relationship with your father, he tries to steer you to do better than he did; more than likely, you are not interested in following in his footsteps. Your mother may tell you to do better than your father, but what does that mean to you? She may even get other so-called successful black men to talk with you about making something of yourself. You ask yourself, "Why are they telling me this when I have twelve years before I'm eighteen?" You say to yourself, "I can't drive, I just started school, so why are they worrying me about this school nonsense?"

~The Playground~

THE BELL RANG and it's time for recess. You head outside to show off your skills; this is your environment. You are the king of the jungle on the basketball court or kickball field or softball field. You may even set up a race to show them how fast you are. You challenge the boys in your class and other classes to a race… you get a few who say they will race you and you all tell one of the girls to stand by the light pole and hold her arms up. You tell everyone the running rules, and you all line up on a line made by one of the boys with hard shoes who dragged his right heel along the dirt and grass. Some of the other kids yell out, "They going to race, y'all."

The girls and boys line up on the sides of the field until you all can't see the girl who is holding up her arms to start the race. Y'all yell at her to move so that you can see her after everyone stretches by tying their shoes and kicking their legs out. Then y'all take your mark and then someone shouts out to the girl, "Tell them to start." She yells out, "YOUR MARK—GET SET—GET READY—GO!" and flings her arms down. You take off as fast as you can and you see that you have competition; the boy named Antwon can really fly. You give it your best, but by the time you get close to the girl, Antwon has already finished. Antwon dusted you, but you came in second and the other kids think that you are all right because you were able to keep up with the fastest boy in their neighborhood.

Your aggressive nature tells you that you have to beat him in something so that you can rule as the king of the school. It won't be doing better in school than him because that's out of the question... who cares if you make a C and he makes a D? That's not impressive. You tell yourself over and over that you have to be good in something, so you focus your efforts on getting better on the basketball court or football field. You are going to beat him in something, just wait...

What if you're not good at sports and don't want to embarrass yourself on the courts or field? After you saw Antwon run like a deer and Marcus handle a basketball like Carmelo Anthony, then you tell yourself that you can't compete with them but can get attention another way. You can be cool by being the class clown... .you don't think of it as a class clown but think of it like being a comedian on stage-you can joan on Mrs. Washington or Mrs. Downing and show the other kids that you're cool. You can make them laugh, you can make them feel good, and you can make them think of you differently. The punishment from the teacher for joaning her or one of your other classmates is a small price compared with making a name for yourself; so you joan on Mrs. Downing.

Mrs. Downing yells at you, "You think that's funny, don't you? We will see if it's funny after you go to the office" and she tells you to follow her.

Your heart is pumping; the kids in the class are laughing softly. You feel somewhat afraid but you're on top of the world because all eyes are on you as you stroll out of the classroom. You are saying to yourself, "Everyone knows who I am" and at the same time trying to come up with a lie to cover your butt when you get suspended or sent to detention. What you haven't asked yourself is: "Are they laughing at me? Or with me?" Do you know the difference? If they are laughing with you, then they think what you did was cool and brave. But most of the time they are laughing at you, and that means that they thought what you did was funny but stupid.

STOP **Here is the kicker: you have definitely formed an impression in the teacher's mind and believe me, she is going to let the other teachers know that you are a clown. Until you move or graduate from that school, you will not be able to undo the clown impression.**

You may not be one who joans on folks to get attention. You may be the person who slumps in his seat as if he doesn't care, falls asleep, daydreams or just doesn't try. You don't think much of this behavior because you ain't causing no trouble, you just ain't trying... so what? Who are you hurting? You! This type of behavior is what I see and hear about most commonly from upset parents... the "don't care" attitude. You have the "don't care" attitude because you have been conditioned to think that you cannot achieve at the level as other people.

~The First C~

THE FIRST DAY of grade school your mother told you to do your best in school and bring home As and Bs. You want to please your mother as well as your relatives. Remember, you have been conditioned to think that sports are what black boys like you are good at, but at the same time you want to make your folks happy. You initially try, but you notice that some of the girls and white boys happen to know more than you do.

When the teacher asks a question, they immediately raise their hands; if she needs someone to lead the group she picks someone other than a black boy. You are young, but you notice that the black boys don't get selected to do some of the neat stuff. You hear the teacher praise a couple of students about how well they do with their work, but it's rarely a black boy. The white boys and girls tell you that their parents do this or do that; you don't know what it is and they don't know either, but it seems important. You try, but it's hard sometimes to keep up; you want to be included so you raise your hand the next time the teacher asks a question even though you don't know the answer.

She looks at you with surprise and says "Darius, what's the answer, sweetie?" and you feel great because all eyes are on you and then you stand up proud, with your chest out and blurt out the wrong answer. The teacher looks at you with a half frown and half smile and says, "No, Darius, that's not correct. Susie, do you know the answer?" And she yells, "Yes, ma'am" and gives the correct answer to the teacher.

You slump down in your chair, embarrassed, and the other kids stare at you especially the ones you think are smart. At that moment, you wish you had kept your hand down. You feel really dumb.

Your teacher doesn't want to call on you again because she doesn't want to embarrass you, so she gives you something that she thinks you can handle—such as being in charge of wiping off the chalkboard—to lift your spirits. What you don't know is that she has formed an impression of you, regardless of her color. More than likely, she is not going to push you or see the potential in you.

STOP **What should you do? You should continue to try, remember, it's just like any sport such as basketball... when you have an open shot you miss the basket half the time during a game, but you don't stop shooting, do you? No! You continue to shoot because you're open, and eventually it will go in. It's the same thing in academics. You won't get it right all the time, but you keep on practicing until you get it right, an A or B.**

You are struggling in a couple of your classes, but are passing. Your mother may not have time to help you because she is so exhausted from working fifteen hours a day. You don't seek help because you are in the first grade; you are just glad no one yells at you about your classes. If you have a father around, he also does not have the time to spend with you on your classes because he had a long day and what's the fuss, you're just in the first grade. You still are not giving up. You want to be recognized and called on during class and want more responsibility than wiping the chalkboards.

Its grade time and you have two Cs, one in math and one in reading; you have a B in art an A in PE.

Your first C, you think not bad. But your mother is initially pissed because you know how to count and know some addition and according to her you can read OK, heck, you are a smart kid. You don't know what the fuss is, but you now know that a C is OK but not so good. Your mother continues to fuss, but over time she rationalizes that it's OK and that you will get it sooner or later. She may never schedule a conference to meet with your teachers because she is so busy. Remember, you have football practice and it's important that she get you there on time 'cause coach said he will not play or start you if you show up late. You continue on the same pattern for another six weeks, and then the bomb is dropped on you.

Midway through the year it's student recognition day, the day that students are recognized for their attendance and academics. You missed a day of school and made a couple of C's, so your parents did not receive a special invitation to come because you weren't going to be recognized. However, your mom plans to attend because you will be one of the trees during the Christmas play right before they hand out the awards. You were not chosen for a speaking part, just a freakin' tree; all you have to do is just stand there and everyone will think you are so cute.

The event occurs and you stand on the stage, bored to tears, while the little white boy who is playing one of the wise men speaks his part and the little black girl who accompanies Mary says a couple of lines and everyone cheers and claps. Afterward, you and your black buddies walk off stage as a tree, a sheep, a star, or whatever they dreamed of for you to act while not saying a word.

Your mother is proud of you because you are her son. You take off that ridiculous costume and sit down with the rest of your classmates. The head teacher in the first grade calls on selected students to come and receive their attendance awards; there are blacks and whites who go up and get their awards, but here is where it really hits you. She now calls on the students who made the honor roll, and you notice that out of the thirty or so kids called up, there are only four blacks: three black girls and a black boy. You don't really know the black boy because he keeps to himself and dresses kinda weird, in your mind. You ask your buddies about him and they say he is a bookworm. They say he ain't all that, 'cause he can't play no ball. You shrug it off, but in the back of your mind you begin to feel that that is the way it's supposed to be. You and your buddies begin to think that the white girls and white boys and a few black girls are the smart folks. You now feel that making As and Bs is not so important, or feel like it's impossible since the people who got called up are smart. You begin to diminish or marginalize your own intellectual ability; you doubt your ability to compete with them.

The moment has an effect on your mother; she too begins to think that you may not be as smart as some of the other kids. She saw only one black boy receive an award and he looked kinda goofy, so she tells herself that she would rather have you well rounded than to look so goofy and out of place up there with those white folks. She rationalizes that since you play sports and make OK grades, then you are doing fine. She is not going to come down hard on you anymore because she can accept a C or two.

You may be the kid who received the academic award. You may be the one who feels the loneliest because they say you talk funny and act weird. You may or may not play sports, but you don't really hang with anybody too tough. You don't talk funny and you don't speak "proper"; you just happen to speak correct English and would rather not talk in slang language. You know, there's absolutely nothing wrong with you...you continue to do your work and speak correctly but whatever you do, you don't look down on other folks or think you are better than your black classmates.

You have the most pressure placed on you because you will soon be moved to classes where you are the only black male and will feel you are out there by yourself. Don't be discouraged or get depressed; there were many others who successfully went through what you are about to face. As a matter of fact, many of the blacks who were the first to go to white colleges in the South were isolated all day long by white students.

~Where's My Dad?~

I DON'T KNOW, but you might have been seven or eight or maybe even younger when you noticed that your father wasn't there. You may have a father who lives in your house, but you don't see him that much because he works all the time. You may not even know who your father is, or maybe you've seen him once or twice. I say this because over half, say 63 percent, of black families are headed by single moms. You may have a father who lives with you, and the two of you may have a great relationship... that's great.

I want to focus on the young men whose fathers don't stay in the same house as them and their mother. You say to yourself, "Where in the heck is he?" Your mother occasionally slips and says something that doesn't sound right. You see your mother working her butt off to get you all the things that you want, but you just don't know how lonely and tired she is. She doesn't want you to go without, so she works part-time jobs or hustles the pyramid businesses to try to make some extra income. She wants to compensate for your father not being there by overburdening herself to get you involved in every activity under the moon.

You are getting up in age and begin to notice things that women do that men don't do. You sometimes feel uncomfortable around her; she notices that you notice as well. You begin to notice that there is a distinct difference between men and women. You take notice of your female classmates and realize that you are stronger than them; you don't cry as easily and you like to be sweaty and sticky.

You now develop a sense of protection for your mother or sister if you have one. You want to be the man of the house; you may even say that you are the man of the house, but you are really not prepared for the task.

You notice some of your friends whose fathers

live with them or are in their lives and you say to yourself, "Where the heck is my father?" It doesn't matter that you see him once a month on the weekend, or only talk with him on the phone during birthdays and holidays, or see him at your sporting events, or ever see him. More than likely, you have a little resentment toward your father for not being there on a consistent basis. You will rarely admit it, but sometimes it shows when you lash out at your mother for no reason or say nasty things about how you wish you stayed with your father.

You may channel your energy elsewhere and feel that you are responsible for all good and bad that happens in your family. You may even feel that since he is not around, it's your mom's fault and start to question everything that she tells you.

You gravitate toward an adult male, maybe your grandfather, church member, coach, or whoever you look up to and sometimes wish they were in your life on a consistent basis. You have man-type questions that need to be answered, but don't quite know how to approach your mom about them. Sometimes, you look at TV and notice a character you think is "straight" and think that you can emulate his look and how he acts. You go to your friends for answers and rely on them to tell you what you already were thinking, regardless if it is the right or wrong answer.

You tell yourself that you will be there for your children no matter what because you don't want your son or daughter to experience what you are going through. You tell yourself that you will be better than the men you've seen come in and out of your mother's life, some who have mistreated her, some who were controlling, some who were threatened by the job she had, and some who were trifling. You may have met one you admired and wanted things to work out, but they just didn't and you can't understand why your mother is still by herself.

Will you honestly remember what you went through, or you are just saying this for the moment? Remember, statistics say that for whatever reason, there are a lot of single black moms raising their kids by themselves. I will tell you to forgive and leave capacity in your heart to love your father if he was not there when he could have been. I will also tell you to never forget the oath that you took to ensure this doesn't happen to the children who you may father.

If you were fortunate to have a father in the house or one who was there for you on a consistent basis, be thankful. If he clothes you, treats your mother fairly, provides for you, and shows you by his actions how to be a man, then emulate all the great things about him. Tell him you love him, even though some people think and say, "Men don't tell other men that they love them." They are wrong as two left shoes and it's OK to tell another man that you love him. This does not suggest that you are gay or a queer. Lastly, when it's your turn, be the example that he was to you and your family or the example that you saw in other men.

~ Flunkin' in Fourth or Fifth~

YOU'VE BEEN on this earth for nine or ten years and kinda know your strengths and weaknesses in the classroom as well as your extracurricular activities (sports/music etc.). You know what you like to eat and what types of movies you like to watch, and you're a little curious about girls. Your mother has given you a little independence; you can walk down the street and play with your friends or stay out in the neighborhood until the streetlights come on. She even allows you a little more flexibility and lets you choose the clothes you wear to school. You somewhat understand conversations between grown folks.

Puberty hasn't hit you yet, but you think you are about grown now. You're not the cute little first grader anymore; you are a veteran at your school. School is now boring, the same ol' stuff, the same ol' smart people from first grade answering all the questions and getting recognized for their science or math projects.

You are doing so-so in school and your mom has gotten used to you making a couple of Cs and a D every now and then. You are involved in music, sports, or some type of activity that really excites you and gets your creative juices flowing. It ain't school, 'cause you can't see how school will benefit you. You figure that when you get in ninth or tenth grade, then you will buckle down and do your work.

You are a cornerback, running back, point guard, forward, shortstop, pitcher, lineman, drummer, trumpet player, artist, DJ, or dancer and you are good at it. You have done some limited research on the successful folks in your field and know that some of them didn't do so well in school and they are successful, so what's the big deal? You know that you can do the work, but why do you have to prove it? Your mother knows that you can do the work as well, but she just doesn't know how to reach you.

You decide the things you are doing after class are more important than school; school is boring. You do care a little about being punished, but it just ain't worth doing all of that work when there are so many other fun things to do. You even say to yourself that you will get the kinda job you want, just wait—you are going to get paid. If Lil Romeo can get paid for rapping, then why can't you do something like that?

You receive your progress reports and find out that you are doing worse than you thought and your mother is going to throw a fit. You know what she is going to say and you know that you will get punished, but it ain't all your fault 'cause you have rationalized that the teacher is out to get you. She don't like people like you; she is always picking on you. You have heard the same ol' stories about not being able to get a good job without college or not being accepted to college without good grades.

Here you go again; you find the few folks who made it big without going to college, and they become your defense for not worrying about school. When someone makes a comment about the future, you say LeBron didn't go to college, P Diddy didn't go to college, 50 Cent didn't go to college, and look at them.

The punishment your mother is going to give you is nothing compared with the image that you have to uphold with the girls and your boys at school. So, taking away your iPod or cell phone or grounding you for a month is nothing compared with your image.

You may have been the goofy kid in first grade or the only black boy in gifted classes, but now you are little more coordinated and have a few friends. Your mom or parents are always on you about doing your best and it's getting old. You don't want to disappoint them and you won't, but at the same time you see other black boys doing all the things they want to do, making Cs, Ds and Fs. You say to yourself that it ain't fair when your mother tells you can't do something or go somewhere because you need to study. You even have the nerve to tell her that it ain't fair that the other kids make bad grades and still do the things they want to do. She tells you something like this, "I ain't worried about them. You are my child or my responsibility and as long as you are in this house, then you will do your best."

You continue to make As and Bs, but just can't see what the big deal is. You hear the stories from other folks about how important education is, but what has it done for you lately, other than made you miss your favorite TV show or a game or not get signed up for a sport? You begin to resent your mom, father, or whoever is preaching to you about good grades because obviously they have not noticed that you make good grades and stay out of trouble. It's if they doubt you or don't trust you.

STOP **They are actually encouraging you, even though they can get pushy. They want you to succeed and know that it is important for you to stay focused; that's their job. It will pay off in the long run, just**

wait. If you follow their guidance, you will be thankful for every TV show or party that you missed.

~Bs, Ho's and Players~

YOU ARE NINE or ten or maybe younger, depending on your maturity. You've noticed that there are differences between women and men. You like sports, but music has captured your imagination as well. Your mom or father may or may not let you watch BET or MTV, but it doesn't matter if they allow you to watch certain music videos. You've been over to your friends' house and seen the videos or turned them on when your parents were outside or you stayed up late to watch while everyone else was asleep. You may not have seen the latest videos; maybe your friends described in detail the moves of the rappers and women dancers, and when you heard the words to the song, you visualized their every move.

More than likely you've seen the videos or heard rap songs such as Jakki Motamouth, "Raw". Your mom or father tells you to turn that mess off when they see you watching it, but because you think you are almost grown you tell them that you don't do that kinda stuff and they are just rapping or dancing.

You notice the grills in the rappers mouth, you notice the baggy pants, you see the gold hanging from their neck, you see them drinking the expensive crystal out of the bottle, you see the twenty-two-inch rims, you see the long shirts with Tupac or Biggie stamped on them. You hear the words they rap; you hear the clean version, but know that is not what they are saying on the uncut version. You see how young they are and how everyone idolizes them. You tell yourself that they are straight and that you would like to trade places with them, but you know your mom wouldn't go for that.

You try to act like them, dress like them, and be like them, even though your mom and dad told you that they really don't own the jets, the houses, and cars. Your mom or dad told you that the few who became rich are the lucky ones and you would be better off getting your lesson and having a decent job than pursuing some pipe dream. They tell you that the life associated with rapping is a fast life straight to jail or the grave, but you see it as being real, sticking it to the man, talking about the man, and doing what a man does to survive.

In your mind, you begin to think they are really keeping it real and expressing the life of a black man. You even have the nerve to look down at black men who work an honest job to support themselves and their families. You now take notice of the few words they say and think that violence is a way of life; think that degrading women is the way it should be; think that partying, drinking liquor, and staying up all night is the life; think that a real man has a rap sheet; think that all police are corrupt; and think that everyone is against you, especially the man, that is, the white man.

You see the videos, hear the clean and uncut versions, and know that women get no respect in most of the songs. They are usually referred to as bitches, ho's, tricks, or something like that. You see the rappers or their posse with a pretty, fine, black woman in tight pants or a bikini dancing all around them. She is posing and showing every feature that excites you and other boys while he dances, raps, or poses calmly and points at her like that is his stuff. She may even bend over to show her butt or shake her butt while he stands behind her and grinds her like a dog or may gesture like he is spanking her.

You think it's cool. You think that he has it going on and then you begin to say the words that your mom warned you not to say. You begin to call your buddies, if you haven't started already, "nigga" and females in your school "bitches, ho's, and tricks." You don't think much of it 'cause you don't mean any harm; it's what they say in the video. You become bolder and that becomes your language when you are at the mall, on the train, on the bus, or at the game. By calling the girls those names, you slowly begin to see them as less than someone who should be respected, especially the ones who don't have a problem with you referring to them as a ho, bitch, or trick.

You even think Tupac and Biggie Smalls made an impact on our society and were as big and influential as Malcolm X or Martin Luther King. Truth told, both were talented, but neither made a significant impact on society other than warn us of the dangers involved in the rap music industry… don't believe the hype!

STOP **You say to yourself, "What's the big deal? They are just expressing themselves, and rap is a way of doing that." I believe you are talented if you can make words rhyme while telling a story. Some rap artists are truly gifted, but some rap music doesn't make a bit of sense, sends no positive information to its listeners, glorifies disrespect to authorities, and degrades women. That music is counterproductive to society, especially the black male.**

Again you say, what's the big deal? Imagine your sister bending over while your favorite rapper grinds on her and refers to her as a bitch, ho, or trick and tell me if you

are all for it. Better yet, picture your mom, big mama or nana shaking their thang or lying on a car with their legs wide open while your favorite rapper pours crystal over her breast and butt. If that don't get you, then picture some man or your mom's male friend greeting her with "What's up, ho?" Remember, you don't like to see your mother dance and definitely won't teach her any of the latest dances that girls your age do, such as poppin'.

You have been conditioned throughout your life that you are a playa; no one intentionally did it, but it is through our culture that we encourage young black boys to have many girlfriends. Your uncles, aunts, big mama, older cousins always inquired about "the girls." When you were young, remarks were made about your looks and that all the girls were going to be after you. When you got older, the first couple of things your relatives said when they saw you were: "How are you doing in school?" and "You gotta girlfriend?" You may have even overheard some of the grown-ups making comments about how handsome or good

looking you were, and you took those comments to heart.

The theory that you are a playa is reinforced when you watch the videos and see the rappers, some of them straight up ugly with many beautiful women, and you think that is the way it is supposed to be. You may even see or hear about your uncle who has multiple girlfriends and notice how he handles his business and think that is the way it is supposed to be.

STOP **You don't have to live up to an image. Be you and reject what you see on TV as reality.**

~That Tingling Feeling~

YOU WERE EIGHT, nine, or maybe ten when you took notice of the young girls in your school. You didn't see them as buddies anymore; you saw them as pretty creatures who needed a strong boy like you to protect them. The girls at that age were more mature than you were and they had crushes on the older boys. You didn't stand a chance of going with them, but you wanted to give it a shot anyway.

You are aware of your body and notice that there are distinct differences between you and the girls. Your mother tells you to get out of the room when she is changing or taking a shower. It's confusing because a few years ago, you were allowed to be in the same room when she was doing these things.

You noticed at an early age that you got an erection in your penis if you rubbed against something, lay on the floor, or fantasized about a pretty woman. You may have even masturbated or had a wet dream and didn't know if it was normal, OK, or what.

STOP Many of the things mentioned are OK and normal; however, you should talk with your father, a man who you trust, or your mom to discuss these issues further.

You are older now and interested in girls. There is a girl in another class who is pretty, smells good, and is smart. You want her to be your girlfriend. When you are around her, she makes you feel good inside. You get a tingling feeling, not a nasty feeling but a good feeling that makes the hair on your arms and legs stand up straight. You get her phone number and you text her or call her at night. She is interested in you as well, and the two of you make a commitment to be boyfriend and girlfriend.

You come back to school, feeling you are on top of the world. You may even point her out to your mother when she drops you off at school. You plan to meet the girl at the movies and showcase her off to the other kids you know. Then the bomb hits you.

Your buddies tell you about some girl they are "hitting" and brag about not being virgins anymore. You are a virgin but don't want to look like no punk and want to fit in, so when they ask you if "you hit that already" and you tell them either "yep" or "I'll hit soon." You know inside that you have no intentions of doing that, all you wanted to do is to kiss her, talk with her on the phone, and hang out with her at the movies or game.

The pressure is on now because they are going to constantly ask you if you "hit that" and, if you are not careful, you will fall into the trap of trying to prove to your friends that you are a man. What you don't know is that most of them ain't hit nothing; they were just talking and bragging 'cause they saw you with your pretty girlfriend. You're in a real big dilemma now. What should you do?

STOP **You should tell them no, you ain't hit it, and you don't have to prove nothing to them. Having sex does not make you a man. Not only can you get her pregnant, but you also could contract a disease and that ain't cool.**

Remember, you have plans for the future and college is in those plans, not a job straight after high school. The responsibility of having a baby is tough for two grown folks, and for a person at your age it is life altering.

If you haven't had this happen, then maybe you've been in a situation where your boys tell you something like this: "After school, meet us over to DiAnthony's house 'cause we are going to run this train on this girl." A train is when more than one boy/man takes turns having sex with a girl/woman. You might ask why a girl or woman would allow several people to have sex with her at one time. The answer usually is because her self-esteem is so low that she sees this as a way to please other folks and get attention. What are you going to do when faced with this situation? Are you going to go along with your boys and participate?

STOP **Or are you going to be responsible enough to tell them that you don't want no part of it? Better yet, will you be man enough to try to talk your friends and the girl out of it? Do you realize that if you participate in that type of activity, it could be considered rape and you and your buddies could face jail time? Plus, it just ain't cool; that's somebody's sister or daughter, and you certainly wouldn't want any of your friends degrading your sister.**

Peer pressure is a mother... however, there is nothing wrong, gay, queer, or faggish about being a virgin. As a matter of fact, it's honorable to be a virgin and focus on being a responsible young man. Ask the fourteen-, fifteen-, or sixteen-year-old who has fathered a child if it's cool trying to raise a baby at that age.

~The Fight~

YOU ARE AGGRESSIVE; that's your nature. You are fast, strong, and ain't no punk. Nobody's gonna "dis" you, 'cause you got pride and folks are gonna respect you. Maybe you like messing with folks and don't take no mess off nobody. You have a reputation to keep up; you feel like you don't get respect, and people better know who they are dealing with when it comes to you.

Somebody says something to you that the other kids think is funny and it pisses you off. You can't believe you got dissed in public, and you can't let that happen without them feeling the consequences. What are they going to think about you now? People won't respect you anymore; they will run all over you.

You ball your fists up and the thought of knocking the living daylights out of them comes across your mind but then… you think about getting suspended and trouble from your mom.

You tell yourself that you are defending your honor, pride, and dignity, and in a split second, you rush him with a punch to the face and the two of you scrap it out.

STOP **That was about the stupidest thing you could have done. I know you hear it all the time about fighting, but what's the point? So what if he called you a name, so what if he dissed you? I guarantee you that it won't be the last time you get dissed. Now you are suspended, marked by the other teachers and principal as a troublemaker, and in trouble with your mom. If he dissed you and it was funny, then let him know "You got me" and keep on going. It will hurt, but you will get over it. Believe it or not, your true friends will respect you and more than likely they will be the ones who will tell him that wasn't cool. If you fight because you are trying to have the back of your boy or because they disrespected your boys, what's the point? You have to**

go through life by yourself and your boys won't always be there for you, so let them deal with their own struggles.

You may be the one who cracked or joaned on the boy in the hall and everyone erupted in laughter. Or, you may be the one who feels that you have to make an example of one of the weaker boys to get your point across… that you demand respect.

You like to brush up against the weaker boys in the hall or the geeky ones and then say, "Why you running up on me?" or "What's your problem— you trying to start something?" You know all along that you are trying to start something, so if that doesn't get them, then it's the name calling. You call them punks or whatever you can think of. You are just waiting for them to bow up or say something back so you can knock the living you know what out of them.

STOP **If you continue that thinking, then you will run across someone who may be weaker but has an equalizer—a gun. More**

importantly, what are you trying to prove? You are showing your weak nature... you actually think your size and strength make you a better person, but they don't. You don't have to display your strength and size for people to respect you. Your classmates will respect you just for who you are if you show respect.

~Smellin' Yourself in Seventh~

YOU ARE NOW twelve or thirteen and the world is changing, so it seems. You are considered a teenager; you have been given more responsibility and you may even be trusted to stay at home by yourself for limited periods of time or trusted to cook on the stove. You are definitely interested in girls and may have had a girlfriend.

Puberty, the life-changing event, occurs. In health class, they talked about the changes boys and girls go through during puberty, but this ain't no class now, this is really happening to you and you want to know what to do next.

Your feet get longer, you grow taller, you grow pubic hair, you grow hair on your face, your voice cracks and deepens, you grow hair under your arms, and your breast becomes sore from the change in your chest. These changes are outwardly noticeable, but there are two other changes that turn you from a boy to a potential man. You can now father a child, as you are informed by your health teacher; however, this does not make you a man. You also have an attitude change and, in most cases, you mentally catch up with your body.

If you are unsure about the changes that are going on in your body, talk to your father or another man you trust. Believe me, they will understand and give you much better guidance than your boys.

You view things differently now; some of the games you used to play are childish now and some of the things you use to giggle at are not funny anymore. Because you can make life and because you are stronger and taller than your mom, you really begin to think that you are a man. If your father does not live with you, then you want to take charge of the house. That doesn't necessarily mean that you want to help out; it just means that you want to be able to boss other folks around.

Your mother is aware of your size and strength, but is not afraid of you. As a matter of fact, if you try to act Billy bad, she will fight you like a man. If you're unfortunate to get a whippin' by your mother, you know that the whipping really doesn't hurt, but the inner pain from disappointing her does.

You test your manhood with her by staying out past your curfew, going places she told you not to go, and doing the ultimate by balling up your fist at her if she tells you to do something that you don't want to do. You may even get crazy and curse under your breath at her if she doesn't let you go to the game or skating rink. You may get stupid and curse out loud and when she yells at you; you may tell her that you don't care or make some nasty remark to her. After she tells you off and makes you feel like a little boy, she says something like this: "You smellin' yourself."

In society's eyes, you are now considered dangerous because you may have the strength of a man or may have the intellect of a genius. You could potentially be a nuisance to society or you could be an economic threat to the establishment.

Don't fall in the trap that so many of our black boys do of being a nuisance to society. The ones who fall in the trap fail to see the power of the mind and only see the damage and destruction they can do with their physical attributes. The survival of the fittest or surviving in the jungle has nothing to do with your aggression, strength, speed, or agility but has everything to do with your character, work ethic, and willingness to apply what you learned.

STOP **Regardless of how you are doing in school, there will be a time when you will challenge your mother's or parents' authority or think about challenging their authority. Remember, you don't pay the light bill, cable bill, gas bill, phone bill, mortgage, or any other bill in the house. Being a man is much more than being able to father a child; a boy can father a child. Being a man is being responsible, respectful, considerate, and, most importantly, self-sufficient (paying all bills to support yourself).**

If you don't meet that criteria, then you need to keep your mouth shut, do your lesson, listen to your mom, and do what she tells you to do. When you become a man, then you can set the rules for your house. Finally, make sure you take a shower daily, put some deodorant on, follow the rules of the house, and stop "smellin' yourself."

~The Misunderstood One~

YOU MAY HAVE been the kid who just didn't fit in with any of your male peers. You were the one who was picked last or who didn't get picked at all when it was time to play ball. You might not have cared if you got picked, but stood along your male peers as if you were interested in playing the game… you just wanted to fit in. You may have thought that playing in the dirt or getting dirty was stupid and wanted no part of games that get you dirty.

You were an indoors person, not necessarily a geek but an indoors person who enjoyed watching certain TV shows or enjoyed cooking. You noticed that you weren't as strong as the other boys nor were you developed like the boys who played sports all the time. As you grew older, maybe eight or nine, your mother pushed you more and more to play sports or do things that were boyish. You went along at first, but decided that that wasn't you and you let her know that if she signed you up that you would not participate.

You developed close relationships with girls at your school and understood them better than some of the boys; you all had the same interests in TV shows, computer games, food, and movies. You began to hang out with a group of girls to the point that you had no real male friends. You would hear the things the girls would say about your male peers such as he is "handsome, fine, straight, all that, good looking, etc." However, you never or rarely made a comment about their remarks.

Your mother began to notice that you didn't have many if any male friends, but that you had a lot of female friends. She began to wonder about you and thought that you needed a male role model or more males in your life so that you would do boyish things. You didn't understand

what the big deal was about because you were being yourself.

The kids at school teased you as being a wimp and soft and some even categorized you as being gay. Deep inside, you began to admire the popular boys at your school. Your feelings were not necessarily of resentment but of jealousy and admiration for possibly their athletic ability, their strength, their domination, their ruggedness, and their way of thinking. You were not developed to their level; you did not have their strength and you certainly didn't command that type of respect and admiration from your female friends. Sure, you were buds with your female posse and they were themselves around you, but when they were around certain boys, they displayed a delicate and sensuous side that you otherwise never saw.

The teasing and categorization made you begin to think that an alternative lifestyle was meant for you. The pressure from your mom or dad to play sports or even watch sports would soon go away if they accepted who you were.

STOP There is absolutely nothing wrong with a boy not wanting to get dirty or play sports. There is nothing wrong with him if he wants to watch sensitive shows or cook or hang out with girls. Men are not determined by how many baskets they score or how many touchdowns they throw or how many girlfriends they have. However, there is an issue with categorizing a person as being gay and there is certainly an issue with a boy allowing someone else to determine that he is gay. Young boy, realize that if you are not as developed or as strong or do not think like some of the other boys, that does not mean you are not meant to be a man or less of a man... your development will come at a later date. Boys develop at different rates, and just because you don't gravitate toward things that your male peers do doesn't mean you are supposed to be gay.

~The Crossroads at Ninth~

YOU HAVE COME to a fork in the road: which way do you go? All of those homework assignments, science projects, and English essays should have laid the foundation for a smooth trip down the right path. While you were in third, fourth, or seventh grade complaining about your homework and boring classes, you should have been learning that information so that your trip down the right path would be a breeze. If you didn't get your lesson then, you have come to the crossroads without a map and will have to try to navigate through the minefields without getting blown up.

Remember when I told you that Mrs. Downing didn't understand you? Well, you probably had some other teachers like Mrs. Downing but just didn't know it. If you "skated by" (you were passed from one grade to the next or were, as the educators call it, socially promoted) you missed out on the foundation necessary to excel on the standardized tests that many colleges rely on for admission.

If you skated by, then you may have had a Mr. Baker or Mrs. Ascott who felt sorry for you and bought into the theory that you couldn't compete or keep up academically with the other kids. Here are some ways to know if you skated by:

1. You were overlooked during class while they were pushing other students to do better, meaning the teachers got upset at some students if they didn't do as well on a test as they expected.
2. You received your D or low C without any encouragement to do better.
3. They looked surprised if you made a high score on a test; some may have thought that you cheated.

4. They talked about enrichment courses and college choices to the other kids, but didn't talk to you about them.

STOP Wake up! In most cases, they are not trying to hurt you; it's been conditioned in them through statistics and what they see and hear on TV or read in journals. As soon as you demonstrate a no care attitude or don't try, then as long as you behave you will be passed from one grade to the next until you are cycled right out of high school without a chance of going to college. Don't buy into the theory or intellectual inferiority. You are just as important and just as smart as Christie or Dakota; apply yourself and you will see. Tell the teacher you are interested in college or college enrichment courses and ask her to give you some advice. If she doesn't tell you what you want to hear, then ask a teacher or adult you respect for his or her advice. As I told you earlier, the largest percentage of folks in slow classes are black

boys and the smallest percentage of folks who attend and get a degree from college are, you guessed it, black boys.

For most public schools, ninth grade is when they begin keeping track of your records/grades to count toward a final average. That average, along with your behavior and your SAT scores, lets college folks know if you are college material. In today's society, if you don't have a college degree, it will be hard to make a decent living because there just ain't that many jobs out there that pay decent money without a college degree or skill such as a plumber, electrician, etc.

By now, one of every seven of your black male peers across this nation has been arrested or had a run-in with the law. You are at the crossroads, and the light bulb is already on, will come on, or will stay off. If you laid a good foundation by making good grades in elementary and middle school, then the next couple of years won't be so difficult. If you haven't laid a good foundation and the light bulb comes on, then you have a chance to navigate to the finish line. Regardless, if the light comes on when you enter the ninth or if the light is already on, don't let anyone tell you that you are not college or trade school material. If you had bad grades in middle school, they will automatically assume that you cannot achieve, but here is where you can prove them wrong. You are already behind in the race but believe me, if you try extremely hard, you can catch up with the rest of the students and go to college.

I probably didn't tell you this earlier, but the finish line is not a high school diploma; it's earning a college degree or obtaining a skill. Many of the factory jobs and jobs that pay decent wages have gone overseas. Even trying to get a job at McDonald's, Popeyes, or Burger King is difficult because many immigrants have taken those jobs.

Your options are wide open if you have a degree; it won't guarantee you a job, but it does get your foot in the door and gives you an advantage over a person who does not attend college. If the light bulb is off, meaning you still don't understand the importance of the next few years, then you will probably regret it in the future. These next four years could determine your status in life. They could determine such things as income, job, lifestyle, exposure to the world, health, spouse, and materialistic things. Here is the kicker: a person with a college degree will earn over $640,000 more during a lifetime than a person without a college degree.

STOP **You may wonder how the next four years can determine your health status in life. If you are not focused and don't take advantage of your education and further yourself, then you probably will not end up with a job that has the best health care plan. McDonald's, Burger King, and other low-paying jobs don't have great health plans. As a black male, you must realize that out of all the races and genders in this country, black males are the shortest lived and most endangered. Because of the issues you will face in life, stress, and the foods that we as blacks love to eat, you will be more susceptible to deadly diseases such as high blood pressure, cancer, and diabetes... believe me, I know.**

~Spiritual Conflict~

MORE THAN LIKELY you've attended church more than a couple of Sundays. You understand what's going on in the world and in your community, but you just don't see what's all the hype from folks who go to church all the time. At this age in your life, if you are blessed with an able body, you feel invincible and just can't relate to those old folks telling the congregation about their issues. Sometimes it's depressing to hear the problems from various folks and then hear the minister talk about all the things you can't or are not supposed to do.

You've heard the messages from the minister about how this life on earth is short, but that never registers with you because you are young and energetic and have the world to conquer. You see more women than men at church and at times wonder why that is so. You have some respect and admiration for the dedicated men in your church, but being a Sunday school teacher, deacon, elder, or committee chairman is something that you just can't see yourself doing in the future; it doesn't pay and it ain't glamorous.

There is a conflict in you, and that conflict has to do with what you've heard from the minister and what you want to do that is considered wrong. There may be a conflict in you because you don't have a problem following the teachings of the Bible, but the pressure of living up to an image for your boys causes you to be one person on Sunday and another during the week. You may even be ashamed of telling your boys that you go to church and like it.

Religion can be confusing because you see the music artists, actors, and athletes dedicating their awards to a higher authority or God but sometimes their action on the field/court, on the movie screen, and on the songs seem contradictory to your minister's teachings. Although you are young, you wonder about the meaning of life and sometimes envision yourself making a difference in the world. Over time, you've become numb or confused about religion because you see everyday people bringing their issues before the church, you see the contradiction in what people say and do, you don't see many men at church, and the image of a godly boy just ain't cool in the eyes of your friends.

STOP **All people make mistakes, and if you heard your minister, then I'm sure he talked about forgiveness. Heck, if you take mental notes and listen to the folks who make their confessions, then you might be able to avoid some of their mistakes. You should never be ashamed of going to church and telling your friends that you do. Don't get discouraged about what people say and then do, I learned at an early age to never put all my faith in a human being, and neither should you... we are all human and will make mistakes.**

~Work Ethic~

BY NOW, YOU kinda know what you want to be or do in life. You've narrowed it down to something that you think you will enjoy doing to earn a living. If you did your lesson and made good grades without your mom or dad on your back, then you have come a long way in establishing a work ethic. You may have been sheltered from doing a lot of chores around the house because your mom or dad wanted you to concentrate on school and other activities. Your mom or dad unintentionally may have conditioned you to look at certain jobs as beneath you.

We in the black community have somehow categorized low-paying and hard-working jobs as jobs we don't want; however, you have to start somewhere. Ain't nothing wrong with flippin' burgers or waiting on tables; what's wrong is if you don't give it 100 percent while you are on the clock. Jobs such as these are honorable and should not be looked upon as your endstate, but a point in your life that you must travel through to get to the job of choice. Flip burgers, wait on tables, bus tables, wash dishes, or whatever's out there that is legitimate, and give 100 percent of your effort. If you follow my guidance, you will be humbled and will soon see the importance of an education.

Your generation of black males will face more difficulties than my generation and previous generations when it comes to employment. My generation of moms and dads have done everything in our power to make life easy for you but as a whole have failed to get across the importance of education and a work ethic. More than likely, you didn't have to cut your own grass or cut the grass in your neighborhood to earn money. More than likely, you didn't have to work during the summer assisting the carpenters or bricklayers on a construction site or work with the landscapers or do some of the back-breaking jobs. It's interesting to note that those jobs were available for me and others but are now gone because immigrants have taken them. That should alert you of the competition you will face for a job.

You think you realize how hard your mom or dad works, but you have no clue what they go through to make ends meet. All you know or think is that you will be able to obtain the same things they have plus more... you tell yourself, just wait till I get out of this house and I will prove it to them. I've seen and know a lot of black boys who were not prepared, who said the same thing, and they will quickly tell you after they get out of the house that trying to make it on their own was no joke.

I know that you want to work, because you want to upgrade your phone plan or get those Nikes or pants or shirt or whatever. You want to make money and you want a job at the mall or somewhere that's not hard. If your mom or dad allows you to get a job, then I challenge you to get one that is hard work, preferably outdoors. If you do a back-breaking job and stick with it, then you will soon come to realize that there is a better life out there for you. You will then concentrate on your lesson because you will see that the folks who are giving the instructions are not doing the back-breaking jobs but are the ones who have been educated past high school.

~The Athlete~

PUBERTY HAS PAID OFF, and you are the size of a big-time athlete or have the skills of a big-time athlete. Or, you could be just an average player but be good enough to make the varsity squad. Because you are an athlete, you are stereotyped not because you're black but because you're a male athlete. Most of your teachers will think that you will use football, basketball, baseball, track, or whatever sport to get over in their class. At the same time that they stereotype you, they will also think that you have an advantage over the students who don't play sports; some will even make it hard for you to pass their class.

If you live in the suburbs or a rural area, then more than likely you will have a white coach who doesn't understand you or any of the black players on your squad. It's not that he doesn't care about you; he just has a hard time trying to identify the music, language, and way you think about life. He wants you to conform to mainstream, and that means acting a certain way and dressing a certain way. Your initial reaction is that he is trying to get you to look and act white but that is far from the truth. You get mad and rebellious because in your mind, you ain't sellin' out.

STOP You must realize that pants hanging off your butt, unkempt hair, and degrading/foul music and talk will not allow you to fully assimilate into society. In a couple of years, you will be looking for employment and if you don't know how to dress mainstream, talk, and act, then you might not land the job you want. Remember, you are the minority and the majority rules in a society. That means that you don't have to lose your

identity, but know there is a time and place for everything. At this particular time, you are representing the school as well as the coach. So every now and then, pull out a tie, dress shirt, dress pants, and dress shoes and wear them to school. You will be surprised how your teachers and coach treat you.

You made the squad and think you have some skills whether you start or not. You've looked past college and already see yourself playing pro ball and living life to its fullest. You have dreams, big dreams. Your coach has told you that you have to maintain a certain grade point average to be eligible. Your goal now is simplify to keep yourself eligible because you won't have a social life if you try to do better than eligible and play your sport.

STOP **You are setting yourself up for a huge fall if you think that only playing ball will get you to your goal. What if you get hurt? What if you're not as good as you think? What is your backup plan? If you**

**don't have one, then you need to get one
and the best way is to do much better than
try to stay eligible.**

Because you are an athlete, the girls, both black
and white, know who you are when you walk the
halls. You get attention that the other boys who
don't play sports don't receive. Your mom or dad
won't necessarily tell you who to date, but let
me tell you this much. If you were not the star
athlete or a good athlete, would that girl (black
or white) hang around or go out with you? You
need to always remember that some males and
females gravitate to folks they think are important
and as soon as their popularity is gone, then they
gravitate to someone else who is popular. As an
athlete, you need a sixth sense; you need to know
when people are using you because of what you
can do for them.

If you are a decent player, when you are in tenth
and eleventh grade you will receive or your coach
will receive pamphlets from many of the major
schools. The majority of these schools have not
done any research on you; you were on a mailing
list submitted by your coach or from a local camp

that you attended. Don't get bigheaded; nearly everyone who has some playing potential will receive pamphlets from colleges. If your grades are not up to par, they won't even entertain the thought of talking to you.

After your junior season, you should know if a college will actively recruit you. Always keep your options open, because the ultimate goal is for you to get a college degree; if you are fortunate to make it to the pros that's icing on the cake. Your goal should always be a college degree. Keep your options open, I mean don't look down on historically black colleges and universities (HBCUs) or smaller schools. If you are a really good player and make decent grades, then you will be pressured to go to a major university. Do some research and know what's best for you and your development.

If you are not actively recruited and you think you are a decent player, then ask your coach if he can market you. I say this because when I was stationed in Mississippi, I had a friend of the family who was a starting quarterback for a 4-A school. This young man was a phenomenal person, great character, good student, and had excellent quarterbacking skills; the school's offense was a throwing type offense. His only problem was his height; he was only five foot ten. He led his team to the state championship and they lost to a good team that had a great running game. Both of his receivers received Division I scholarships; however, he was barely recruited.

His coach didn't contact the area HBCUs to see if they needed a quarterback, nor did he do any active recruiting for him. I contacted the HBCUs and they informed me that they would have gladly accepted him; however, they had filled their rosters and thought that he was taken by one of the larger schools. He did end up getting a scholarship, but it shouldn't been so difficult. If your coach won't help, then get someone to tape your games and send your tapes to local colleges. You might be surprised at the responses you get.

If you are fortunate to get a scholarship, always remember three things:

1. Stay grounded and never forget where you came from. There will be a lot of folks pumping you up like you are all that. The folks back home

who made you should be the ones you place first in your life. There will be plenty of young ladies who will flock to you, but have a sixth sense and determine who has your interest at heart.

2. You're in college to earn a degree; playing sports just gives you that opportunity without paying for it.

3. You are a prostitute for four or five years and the college is the pimp for that same period of time. The college owes you absolutely nothing after it has used you on the field, court, or track. You can allow the college to use you by making money from ticket sales and TV revenue by meeting the minimum requirements to stay eligible for those four or five years, or you can let them make their money and you can get a degree to make your money if the pros don't pan out. I hope you choose the latter because there are plenty of black boys who played four years of big-time sports and have nothing to show for it.

~Closed or Open Door at Eighteen~

Open at Eighteen

I HOPE YOU followed your mom's or dad's guidance and turned the light bulb on well before your senior year, or I hope that you continued to do well in school and stayed out of trouble, or I hope that you turned your life around after you realized that you waited too late to get serious about your lesson. Regardless, you are eighteen and still have a future whether the door seems closed or is wide open.

The door will be wide open if you did what your mom or dad said and gave it your very best. You made decent to very good grades, did OK on the SAT, and stayed out of trouble. You now have the option of attending college and you will fill out applications for admission to several of them. Heck, you already know what you want to major in… it's just a matter of getting accepted. You should be burning up with fire of determination now, because you will be on your own pretty soon and you will be executing a plan to be on top of the world. I will tell you that it won't be a cakewalk, but as long as you remember your goal of getting that paper, then you will excel beyond that point.

You also have a chip on your shoulder because people had doubts about you and you want to prove them wrong. They doubted that you would go to college; you remember that you were overlooked or marginalized, and want so desperately to show them up. You also know that there are folks like your mom or dad who believed in you, and you want them to be proud of you. Never give up; do your best, and you will succeed.

Closed at Eighteen

You are the one who skated through school; had the don't care attitude; got in trouble; or maybe got a girl pregnant and became a father at sixteen, seventeen, or eighteen. It seems like a dead end because even though you will receive a diploma or certificate of attendance for twelve years, your options are limited. However, you feel a sense of accomplishment because you are finished with the structured learning environment and are now on your own to do whatever you want between 7:00 a.m. and 4:00 p.m.

What are you going to do? When you go out there looking for full-time employment, you quickly see that the jobs they are talking about are not so glamorous and they don't pay much. They don't even pay enough to buy a house or nice car. You may have to stay with your mom for a couple of years to save up enough money to rent a place of your own. You might not be able to move in a couple of years because Iesha, your baby's mom, has a court order on you to pay child support since you will be getting a full-time job soon. You become bitter because you didn't keep your penis in your pants and didn't listen to them "don't know what they talking about grown folks."

You begin to understand what some of the black men had told you about getting your lesson. You had a part-time job during school and that was cool, but now, looking at a full-time job making minimum wage or even double minimum wage, you soon realize that five to ten dollars per hour won't take you far when you pay FICA, Medicare, state, and federal taxes. You become depressed because you feel that you are better than what they are paying you. You give up and blame the man, turn to illegitimate ways of making money, or make a vow to lift yourself up.

STOP **There are a lot of black boys who choose the illegitimate way of making money and there are a large share who constantly blame the man or the establishment for their predicament even though they had the same opportunities as the few black boys and girls who took advantage of their situation. Your**

mom, dad, and I want you to make a vow to lift yourself up. Although it seems like it, the door ain't closed. Your trip won't be as smooth as the boy or girl who gets a degree from college, but you can get there and exceed them if you put your mind to it. Learn a skill or go to trade school to get qualified in an industry that is short of laborers; there ain't many electricians, plumbers, and carpenters in the black community anymore. The military is an option, and it will pay for your education. Whatever you do, just don't fall in the trap of casting the blame on others. Take charge of your life and make a difference in this world.

~Successful or Scumblin' and Bumblin' at Twenty-five~

Successful at Twenty-five

YOU ATTENDED COLLEGE, a historically black college, and had the best four years of your life and at the same time received a degree in education, business, engineering or whatever. *I encourage you to attend a historically black college, but really want you to attend college and get a degree; I am just partial to the HBCUs.*

You got your first job right after college and are doing well at work. You learned a lot about yourself and know how difficult it is to make it with a college degree and wonder how your friends who didn't go to college make it. You realize that money makes things happen; you realize that there are not many decision-makers of your color, male or female, in your profession; and you realize that you gravitate toward women who have college degrees and are working because you just have more in common with them. You are renting right now but have saved enough money for a down payment on a house and understand the value of home ownership; it is in the realm of possibility at your age because you are getting paid a nice salary.

After four years of living the life in college and after four years of the corporate world, you decide to settle down with a lovely lady whom you've been dating for a couple of years. You are due a promotion and she is doing quite well in her career, and the two of you together can live a good life together so you all decide to jump the broom.

Scumblin' and Bumblin' at Twenty-five

The light bulb still has hasn't clicked on and you're eight years removed from high school. You've had odd jobs that put a little change in your pocket, but don't have a steady source of income. You live with your mom and are responsible for paying the cable bill. She doesn't allow you to bring a woman to the house after certain hours of the day, but you sneak one over every now and then when your mom has gone to work.

You blame all of your problems on the man and the government. You just can't understand why you can't get one of those high-paying jobs that some blacks are hustling to every morning. Your classmates who earned a degree from college and are doing well are snobbish in your mind, and you have rationalized that you don't want to be considered a token negro; you want to get paid but keep it real at the same time. You've become like Baby Boy: materialistic, lazy, looking for a quick dollar instead of working hard, and thinking you're a man 'cause you fathered a child.

In the movie *Baby Boy*, Baby Boy's mama's boyfriend made a profound statement. He told

Baby Boy that the problem with him and his generation of black males is that they didn't know what guns and butter meant and the difference between the two. He went on to say that butter represented the things that they focused on such as cars, TVs, jewelry, and other things that don't appreciate in value, while the white man has the guns, that is, stocks, bonds, houses, and other things that appreciate.

Your vision of the future is a dream that will probably not come true unless you put some sweat equity (hard work) in it to make it happen. Since you can't afford a place of your own, can't afford a wife or family, and don't have money on a consistent basis, you now rely on being a playa to make up the difference. You lean on women to help you pay your phone bill, car insurance, and groceries and to provide spending change. In your mind's eye, you're all that, but in society's eye, you are a trifling, scumblin' and bumblin' negro.

~High School Reunion~

TWENTY YEARS have passed since you walked across the stage to receive your high school diploma or certificate of attendance. You maybe thirty-eight or thirty-nine by now and have aged with time, maybe gracefully or maybe not so gracefully. More than likely you have a family and are focused on your child or children's future. You have lived over half your life and now reflect back on what you did right and what you wish you could change.

You are a lot more cautious than you were right out of high school. You still drive fast, but don't take as many chances; amusement rides still excite you, but your heart and back just can't take some of the rides; you think you can still play ball, but your knees and back just won't hold up for a full game and you now actually take notice of the outdoors.

All the things that your mom, dad, and relatives warned you about are now coming true. The staying up late at night has caused wear and tear on your body; the drinking has affected your internal organs; the fried foods and excessive salt and sweets have caused your blood pressure and sugar levels to rise; and the lack of exercise has accelerated all of the diseases that kill black men. Regardless of your condition, time has flown by and your high school reunion is next month.

~Young man with the Light Bulb On the Entire Time~

You are the young man whose light bulb was on and stayed on. You are an executive in your company and you and your wife are doing quite well. You have an all-brick, five-bedroom, three-bath house with a state of the art entertainment room. You have traveled the world and it's nothing for you and your family to fly across the country for a weekend. You and your wife are active in church; as matter of fact, you have been appointed as the building fund chairman because of your business acumen.

You've donated your time and money to many worthwhile charities. You truly feel that you are making a contribution to society. You look at where you started and where you are and want to make a mark in your community. There is not much that you wish you could change. You still carry that chip on your shoulders because you want to continue to prove people wrong about what they forecasted for your future.

You received your invitation to your twenty-year high school reunion, and you and your wife cleared your calendars to attend. You want to see your friends from high school but more importantly, you want them to see how successful you've become. You and your wife show up at the reunion and look around only to see a handful of your friends who made it to the reunion. Out of the seventy black males in your class, only ten attended even though thirty-five still live in town. Everyone is amazed and puzzled to see how you transformed from that geeky-looking boy to a refined corporate executive with a lovely wife. You are loving it because you can feel the jealousy and admiration as you mingle with your classmates. You run into Chris, who skated by in all of his classes and got into trouble every now and then. You didn't think Chris would make much of himself, but are amazed at how he looks and how well he is doing for himself... you are really impressed.

~Young Man Who Finally Figured Out How to Turn the Light Bulb On~

Chris is the boy whose light bulb came on when it was almost too late. Chris barely graduated from high school. He got his stuff together when he was in the tenth grade and couldn't pull his grades up enough to get into college. Chris worked part time and began working full time for a painter after high school. He worked long hours and many weekends to make extra money to pay for his car and apartment.

Chris did OK, but later regretted not going to college or trade school. He saw how much money was made in his business and others by those who owned or managed the businesses. After six years of riding around in the back cab of a Ford truck and painting houses and commercial buildings, not knowing how much money his boss was getting paid for the contracts, he decided to do something about it.

Instead of just being a painter, he enrolled in a community college and took night business classes for a couple of years until he earned his associate's degree. Chris used the knowledge he learned from college and the savings he accrued over the years to start his own painting business. It was rough for him and the couple of painters he recruited, but after a few years he was able to establish a large clientele.

Chris got married to his high school sweetheart a few years after he graduated and they are doing quite well. Chris still paints but now does more management and marketing of his company to draw business. He too has a large house with entertainment room and swimming pool. He doesn't have as much recreational time as his old high school buddy but when he is able to break away from his job, he spends quality time with his family.

Chris received his invitation as well and plans on attending the reunion. Chris and his wife show up to the reunion looking quite nice. The hard labor over the years has aged him in the face, but kept his body in tiptop shape. As he mingles and passes out his business cards, his classmates are astonished that he has accomplished so much.

He too has donated his services to charity and has done a lot in the community to help struggling brothers with employment. All of his classmates admire him because they have heard about the great things he has done in his community. They are more astonished that he is a dedicated family man and churchgoer because he was a hell-raiser in school.

As he looks back on his life, he will be the first one to tell a young black boy to get his lesson and go to college. Even though he is now successful, he reminds his kids of the struggles he went through to get where he is now. Chris enjoys the moment with his wife as his classmates remember him as the scumblin', bumblin' hell-raiser. Today, he is seen as a successful businessman and responsible family man.

Chris chats with a group of classmates, and everyone asks about Octavio. Octavio had the "don't care" attitude in school, fathered a baby in high school, and always stayed in trouble. Someone in the group states that they saw Octavio recently and he didn't look so good. They went on to say that he lived in town and that he was really struggling. You all think about it for a moment and someone whispers, "That doesn't surprise me."

~Young Man Whose Light Bulb Was Never Turned On~

Octavio lives somewhere, with someone, depending on what day of the month. He has been scumblin' and bumblin' since he left high school. He currently works full time at the civic center doing odd jobs at the concession stands. He makes about eight dollars per hour, which nets him about $950.00 per month after taxes. His rent runs him around $300 per month, and his car note is about $200 per month. After he pays child support and other bills, he has about $125 remaining for the month. He is one of the highest paid employees at his job, and probably won't receive a pay raise because he doesn't give 100 percent.

He still has a chip on his shoulder and blames the world for his money and career problems. He figures that since he doesn't make that much money, he shouldn't give 100 percent at his job. His thought process is "pay me more and you will get more." However, employers don't think like that; they pay you more because you show potential and work hard.

He has a child by one of his high school classmates and pays her child support each month. He also has a girlfriend and they have a child together as well. His girlfriend really cares about him and helps him out each month by paying a bill or two for him. She encourages him to do his best at his job or go to night school to get his GED so that he can get a better paying job. He always tells her that he will, but just doesn't make the effort to do so.

He is a dreamer who thinks that it is all luck to make it big, so he invests the little money he has into get-rich schemes. The little money he has after bills are paid is spent on the lottery, gambling, and enhancements to his cars. He even thinks that buying rims and detailing his car will make it go up in value. His sense of investment is not a mutual fund, stocks, or savings but butter—cars, TVs, and jewelry.

He received the invitation for his class reunion and can't believe it's been twenty years since he received his certificate of completion. Even though he still lives in the same town, he won't attend because he doesn't feel that he is where he wants to be in life. He has heard about his classmates who finished college or started their own businesses and is deeply bitter and resentful that they were lucky and he wasn't.

Looking back, he regrets that he didn't do better in school but won't admit it to anyone else. After all those years, he still doesn't get it. He thinks it's all about luck and not about hard work and attitude.

~Looking Back~

IT'S REPORTED that 32 percent of black males in the age group twenty to twenty-nine is under some form of criminal justice supervision on any given day. It is reported that a black male born in 1991 has a 29 percent chance of spending time in prison at some point in his life. It's reported that a black male will live 7.1 years less than any other racial group. It's reported that 44 percent of black males are overweight and 24 percent are considered fat. It's been reported that for every six to seven females who attend college there is only one black male who attends. It's been reported that there are more black fathers than black men. It's been reported that if you asked ten black men what they were going to leave their children for an inheritance, seven would tell you bills and debt.

But!!!!... I know you will become the executive or turn the light bulb on (if it's not already on) and become an entrepreneur, manager, supervisor or just a good hard-working employee. I know that you won't disappoint your mom and dad and will make a great contribution to society. I know you will do the right thing by your sistas and never degrade them. I know you will heed the warnings of your mom, dad, and doctor about living, eating, and doing the right things for your body. I know that you respect people for who they are. I know that you will connect with your spirituality and ensure that you are actively helping others. I know that you will not forget where you came from and help someone else when you make it. In the face of adversity, I know that you will not let people tell you to stop trying because they say it's the government or the man's fault for your situation.

I know that you will value home ownership, mutual funds, savings, and stocks and bonds more than you value a car. I know that you will not turn a blind eye to a wrongful situation. I know that you will preach EDUCATION, ATTITUDE, and WORK ETHIC as the black man's equalizer.

There will be a time, if it hasn't come already, when you look back and your remembrance

will either be bitter or sweet, depending on the decisions you made at life's crossroads.

Acknowledgements

I WANT TO personally thank Wilson Russ who inspired me to write this collection of thoughts; this was his brainchild, I just put it on paper. As I look back on my childhood, I wouldn't have made it this far without strong men like my dad, my junior high coaches who were a disciplinary extension of him and the great examples of men at my home church. I along with many other black boys were fortunate to have positive male role models in our life but in today's society that's a rarity; many of the positive male role models are now replaced with the latest rapper, basketball or football star. I certainly don't want to omit the strong women in my life who helped shaped me like my mother and some of the older women of my home church. I, along with many other black males have truly been blessed with parents who guided us in the right direction to make the right decisions which has made us somewhat successful in today's society. I certainly don't want to paint a totally bleak picture because I also know that there are many young black males who have the potential to come along and become even more successful than my generation and others have become; for many, its just a matter of a black male in their life to love them, discipline them, teach them, and guide them… that's what scares me-the positive black male to do just that on a consistent basis.